What Happens at a Party Store?/

¿Qué pasa en una tienda de cosas para fiestas?

By/por Amy Hutchings

Reading Consultant: Susan Nations, M.Ed.,
author/literacy coach/consultant in literacy development/

Consultora de lectura: Susan Nations, M.Ed.,
autora/tutora de alfabetización/consultora de desarrollo de lectoescritura

WEEKLY READER®

PUBLISHING

Please visit our web site at www.garethstevens.com.
For a free catalog describing Gareth Stevens Publishing's list of high-quality books,
call 1-800-542-2595 (USA) or 1-800-387-3178 (Canada). Our fax: 877-542-2596

Library of Congress Cataloging-in-Publication Data

Hutchings, Amy.
      [What happens at a party store? Spanish & English]
      What happens at a party store? / by Amy Hutchings ; reading consultant,
      Susan Nations = Qué pasa en una tienda de cosas para fiestas?/
      por Amy Hutchings ; consultora de lectura, Susan Nations.
           p. cm. — (Where people work = Dónde trabaja la gente?)
      Includes bibliographical references and index.
      ISBN-10: 0-8368-9283-6   ISBN-13: 978-0-8368-9283-3 (lib. bdg.)
      ISBN-10: 0-8368-9382-4   ISBN-13: 978-0-8368-9382-3 (softcover)
      1. Party supplies stores—Juvenile literature.   2. Party supplies stores—
Employees—Juvenile literature. I. Nations, Susan. II. Title. III. Title: Qué
pasa en una tienda de cosas para fiestas?
      HF5469.654.H8818   2009
      381′.456887—dc22   2008013213

This edition first published in 2009 by
Weekly Reader® Books
An Imprint of Gareth Stevens Publishing
1 Reader's Digest Road
Pleasantville, NY 10570-7000 USA

Senior Managing Editor: Lisa M. Herrington
Creative Director: Lisa Donovan
Designer: Alexandria Davis
Photo Coordinator: Charlene Pinckney
Photographer: Richard Hutchings
Translation: Tatiana Acosta and Guillermo Gutiérrez

The publisher thanks Strauss Party Warehouse in Port Chester, New York, for its participation
in the development of this book.

Printed in the United States of America

1 2 3 4 5 6 7 8 9 10 09 08

Hi, Kids!

I'm Buddy, your Weekly Reader® pal. Have you ever visited a party store? I'm here to show and tell what happens at a party store. So, come on. Turn the page and read along.

— — — — — — — — —

¡Hola, chicos!

Soy Buddy, su amigo de Weekly Reader®. ¿Han estado alguna vez en una tienda de cosas para fiestas? Estoy aquí para contarles lo que pasa en una tienda de cosas para fiestas. Así que vengan conmigo. ¡Pasen la página y vamos a leer!

Boldface words appear in the glossary.

— — — — — — —

Las palabras en **negrita** aparecen en el glosario.

Today is a big day! Dan and his mom get ready for his birthday party. They have made a list of things they need.

– – – – – – – – – –

¡Hoy es un día muy importante! Dan y su mamá preparan la fiesta de cumpleaños de Dan. Han hecho una lista de las cosas que necesitan.

They go to a party store. Here they will find things they need for a fun party.

– – – – – – – – –

Dan y su mamá van a una tienda de cosas para fiestas. Allí encontrarán lo necesario para una fiesta muy divertida.

First, the **store clerk** helps them find plates, napkins, and cups. Eight friends will come to Dan's party.

– – – – – – – – –

Primero, una **vendedora** los ayuda a encontrar platos, servilletas y vasos. Dan invitó a ocho amigos a su fiesta.

store clerk/
vendedora

9

Next, Dan finds a **piñata** (peen-YAH-tuh).
A piñata is filled with candy and
small gifts.

— — — — — — — — —

Después, Dan elige una **piñata**. Una
piñata se rellena de caramelos y
regalitos.

piñata/
piñata

11

A **stock person** makes sure the shelves are full. Dan finds **favors** on the shelves. The favors will go in party bags for his friends.

— — — — — — — — —

Un **reponedor** se asegura de que las estanderías estén llenas. En éstas, Dan encuentra **obsequios** para sus invitados. Más tarde, los meterá en pequeñas bolsas que dará a sus amigos.

stock person/
reponedor

favors/
obsequios

13

Then Dan and his mom get the balloons. A worker blows up the balloons with a **helium tank**.

— — — — — — — — —

Después, Dan y su mamá eligen los globos. Una empleada los infla usando un **tanque de helio**.

helium tank/
tanque de helio

15

Dan and his mom are done. Their list is all checked off.

— — — — — — — — —

Dan y su mamá ya han terminado. Han ido tachando todas las cosas de la lista.

The **cashier** adds up how much their things cost. Dan's mom pays the cashier.

– – – – – – – – – –

El **cajero** suma el precio de todo lo que compraron. La mamá de Dan paga al cajero.

cashier/
cajero

19

Dan is so excited! This is going to be his best birthday party yet.

– – – – – – – – – –

¡Dan está muy emocionado! Ésta va a ser la mejor fiesta de cumpleaños que jamás haya preparado.

21

Glossary/Glosario

cashier: a person who takes in and pays out money in a store

favors: small gifts that are given out at a party

helium tank: a container filled with a light gas that is used to blow up balloons

piñata: a decorated container filled with candy and small gifts that is hung up to be broken with a stick by people who are blindfolded

stock person: a person who works in a store and makes sure the shelves are full

store clerk: a person who works in a store

- - - - - - - - - -

cajero: persona que recibe el dinero y da el cambio en una tienda

obsequios: pequeños regalos para los invitados de una fiesta

piñata: objeto hueco de cartón que se rellena de caramelos y pequeños regalos y que luego se cuelga para que una persona con los ojos tapados lo rompa usando un palo

reponedor: empleado de tienda encargado de reponer la mercancía en las estanterías

tanque de helio: contenedor cerrado lleno de un gas muy ligero que se usa para inflar globos

vendedor: persona que trabaja en una tienda

For More Information/Más información

Book/Libro

Cashiers. Katie Bagley and Cher Terry
(Coughlan Publishing, 2001)

Web Sites/Páginas web
Kids Work!/
¡Los niños trabajan!
www.knowitall.org/kidswork
Explore fun jobs in a community by clicking on the different workplaces./
Exploren empleos divertidos en una comunidad haciendo click en los diferentes lugares de trabajo.

ZOOM Party

pbskids.org/zoom/activities/party
Plan a party with fun ideas, crafts, foods, and games that come from kids./
Organicen una fiesta con divertidas ideas, manualidades, comidas y juegos inventados por niños.

Index/Índice

About the Author

Amy Hutchings was part of the original production staff of *Sesame Street* for the first ten years of the show's history. She then went on to work with her husband, Richard, producing thousands of photographs for children's publishers. She has written several books, including *Firehouse Dog* and *Picking Apples and Pumpkins.* She lives in Rhinebeck, New York, along with many deer, squirrels, and wild turkeys.

Información sobre la autora

Amy Hutchings formó parte del grupo de producción original de la serie *Barrio Sésamo* durante los primeros diez años del programa. Más adelante, pasó a trabajar con su esposo, Richard, en la producción de miles de fotografías para editoriales de libros infantiles. Amy ha escrito muchos libros, incluyendo *Firehouse Dog* y *Picking Apples and Pumpkins.* Vive en Rhinebeck, Nueva York, junto con muchos venados, ardillas y pavos salvajes.